DEFECT PREDICTION IN
SOFTWARE DEVELOPMENT
MAINTAINENCE &

DEFECT PREDICTION IN
SOFTWARE DEVELOPMENT
MAINTAINENCE &

KSN PRASAD
ANNALURI SREENIVASA RAO
RUDRA KUMAR

PARTRIDGE

To order additional copies of this book, contact
Partridge India
000 800 10062 62
orders.india@partridgepublishing.com

www.partridgepublishing.com/india

CONTENTS

LIST OF FIGURES

LIST OF TABLES

1

INTRODUCTION

Increasing number of applications, rising complexity, and device connectivity is driving the need for developing qualitative programming. Further, with applications ranging from small operations to complex as high as banking applications, the maintenance costs are expected to be low. Accordingly, the need for accurate fault estimation gains prominence role in achieving both the goals of quality programming and minimal maintenance overheads [1]. Predicting possible faults enables rectification of such faults on a timely basis along with low efforts on maintenance. Several researchers successfully developed detection parameters to identify faults in programs. These parameters together with fault information are used to build sophisticated fault estimation models in the initial stages of programming.

Software Fault or fault prediction (SFP) techniques primarily involve module classification into two categories- fault-prone or non-fault prone. Detection parameters and fault information extracted from earlier versions or a similar application are fed to the proposed SFP model. The model, thus developed is used to classify modules of existing applications into fault-prone or non-fault prone. Programmers can then examine the performance of the model on fault-prone sections in the previous versions of the program. Knowledge gained from weak sections will assist test engineers to fix high fault-prone sections despite limited availability of test resources. Accordingly, without compromising on the quality of the program, low maintenance costs can be achieved in a timely manner.

Multiple models and techniques of fault estimation are proposed in the contemporary literature, which can categorize into two main types- conventional models and machine learning (ML) models. While conventional models are static and rely on regression analysis and estimates of experts, machine learning models are dynamic and continuously update programs with additional data inputs, resulting in a superior performance as time progresses.

Lack of information on the extent of adaption and implementation in the industry poses significant challenges to ML model developers. Despite the east of applying such techniques and prominence of fault estimation [2], limited information on their success in practical applications restricts developers from evaluating the model practicality. Forecast accuracy remains the key parameter for performance measurement of model despite the model performance being dependent on multiple dimensions [3].

2

TAXONOMY

2.1 Program Fault Detection Procedure

Researchers in contemporary literature successfully established evidence to depict the relationship between certain inherent module features such as calling structure and quality of the program. Accordingly, multiple models are suggested evaluating the impact of each of these characteristics and combination of characteristics on model performance [4], [5], [6] and [7]. Figure 2.1 included in the section details the overview of fault detection procedure.

Figure 2.1 depicts fault estimation procedure through ML techniques. Some of these techniques are studied in the references included in [8], [9], [10], [11], [12], [13], [14].

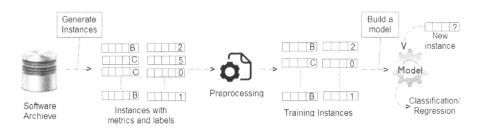

Figure 2.1: The Common process of software defect prediction

The initial phase in building a forecast method is creating instances from various software documents like CVS systems, e-mail files, issue detecting systems, and etc. Every instance represents a system, a package or a system component, a class, a method and a source code archive. In addition, it represents modified the code as per prediction granularity. An instance includes multiple features which are explored from different software files. This instance is defined with the bug count. In Figure 2.1, the generated instances from various software files are represented as buggy "B" Clean "C" or the quantum of faults.

After instance generation with various parameters and labels, most familiar machine learning preprocessing mechanisms are implemented. In particular, feature sampling, data normalization techniques and noise mitigation procedures are highly employed preprocessing techniques for bug prediction studies [15], [13], [16], [17], [18]. However, as depicted in [10], [12], usage of preprocessing techniques is not mandatory in every bug prediction studies. Thus, these techniques are optional.

A prediction method is trained by using the final instances of the training set, as depicted in Figure 2.1. This prediction method can check for a bug in a new instance. The estimation for B or C of the corresponding instance is classified as binary (zero or one) and bug count stands for regression.

2.2 Fault Estimation Parameters

Fault estimation parameters are vital for the construction of any forecasting tool. Typically, the fault estimation parameters are grouped as code parameters or process parameters. The code parameters are obtained from source code and are easy to obtain. Process parameters, on the other hand, are obtained from historical data stored in different repositories including CVS system or tracking systems.

2.2.1 Code Parameters

Code parameters enable researchers to understand the extent of complication in any source code. Code or product parameters function with an underlying assumption that the higher the complexity of a given code, the higher is the probability of the code to contain faults. To evaluate the extent of the complication of the source code, multiple research studies have been conducted.

Size parameters compute multiple dimensions of a program including its length, capacity, and magnitude [19]. Coding lines (LOC) is often used to depict these parameters. Earlier, Akiyama approach was used to estimate faults through LOC [20]. However, LOC concept has been extensively used by several researchers for developing their estimation methods [10], [21], [12], [13], [22], [23].

The study in [24] relied on operators and operands count for building new size parameters. The suggested parameters include difficulty level, resources and time required, language, length and volume [24]. Of this, the majority of parameters are associated with quantity. Similar to Akiyama approach, the Halstead approach is also being used in multiple studies [13], [23], [25].

In [26], the cyclomatic parameter is suggested for calculating program complex nature with the use of control flow graphs. This parameter is calculated through node count, arc count and a number of interconnected components in the code. It depicts the complexity of two control paths. Compared to earlier model in [24], the model does not consider size parameters of the quantity of code. The approach was used in phone networks and other studies for fault estimation [27], [28], [13], [29], [16], [23], [25].

With growing prominence of OOPs programs, code parameters relying on the OOPs concept were also researched for fault estimation. The study in [30] developed the CK parameters for fault prediction, listed in Table 2.1 in this research work.

Table 2.1: CK Metrics [30]

Name	Description
WMC	Weighted methods per class
DIT	Depth of inheritance tree
NOC	Number of children
CBO	Coupling between object classes
RFC	Response for a class
LCOM	Lack of cohesion in methods

CK parameters are built on the features of OOPs concepts like inheritance and cohesion [30]. In [31], researchers evaluated these parameters in their ability to construct an efficient fault estimation model. Later, multiple researchers relied on CK parameters to construct their estimation models [8], [10], [4], [15], [12], [32], [18].

In addition to CK parameters, other OO parameters have also been suggested [33]. The study relied on the quantity of the code. Table 2.2 depicts the OO parameters, which count the instance variables, methods. Some of the estimation models suggested on the basis of OO parameters include [10], [15], [12], [32], [18], [34], [35].

Table 2.2: Example class-level OO metrics
used by D'Amabros et al [10]

Name	Description
FanIn	Number of other classes that reference the class
FanOut	Number of other classes referenced by the class
NOA	Number of attributes
NOPA	Number of public attributes
NOPRA	Number of private attributes
NOAI	Number of attributes inherited

LOC	Number of lines of code in a class
NOM	Number of methods
NOPM	Number of public methods
NOPRM	Number of private methods
NOMI	Number of methods inherited

2.2.2 Process Parameters

The following section provides an overview of process parameters and associated design aspects. Seven process parameters are listed in Table 2.3.

Table 2.3: Representative process metrics

Process Metrics	# of Metrics	Metric Source	Venue
Relative code change churn [14]	8	Version Control	ICSE'05
Change [29]	17	Version Control	ICSE'08
Change Entropy [11]	1	Version Control	ICSE'09
Code metric churn, Code Entropy [36], [10]	2	Version Control	MSR'09
Popularity [8]	5	E-mail archieve	FASE'10
Ownership [9]	4	Version Control	FSE'11
Micro interaction metrics [12]	56	Mylyn	FSE'11

1) Code churn parameters: In [14], researchers suggested 8 code churn parameters (M1 to M8), to calculate the number of alterations in code. For instance, the M1 parameter is calculated through the division of churned LOC (cumulative count of additional lines plus removed lines in revised coding compared to original coding) with total LOC. The rest of the parameters from M2 to M8 compute other changes including the ratio of removed LOC to total LOC,

file alterations to total files etc. The study identified that the churn parameters have high efficiency in estimating code complexity and thereby, fault-proneness.

2) Change parameters: Change parameters compute the number of changes in the revised source code compared to the original source code. Count of specific parameters including the count of changes or revisions or editors of a given code. The study in [29] identified 18 such parameters from storage repositories for comparing different change parameters and their associated complexity estimation. It also counted both newly added and removed LOC as was suggested by researchers in [14]. However, these change parameters ignored the relation of file count to total LOC. Instead, maximum count and average count of these metrics are computed. File age parameters and maximum/ average of change sets are also calculated in the study [29]. Experimental results of the study suggest improved estimation accuracy of change parameters over code parameters.

3) Change Entropy: the study in [11] used entropy to obtain complexity of changes and suggested HCM. To evaluate the efficiency of HCM, researchers used linear regression techniques over HCM or two different change parameters i.e. count of earlier changes and earlier faults. The study was executed on six programs [11]. Evaluation results on these six programs depicted that estimation method incorporating HCM had superior performance compared to two change parameters. The concept of incorporating entropy is new but the concept faces critical limitations. The limitations include that the HCM approach was compared with only the two change parameter concept, exposing the lack of robustness of the proposed model. Further, the execution was made at the sub-system level instead of file-level.

4) Churn parameter and code entropy: In [36], the study compared different fault estimation parameters. For comparing different parameters, separate study introducing churn parameters (CHU) and code entropy (HH) is not done. Instead, these parameters are compared as suggested in [14] and [18]. CDU computes the modification on a 15-day basis of CK parameters or OO parameters.

As it calculates changes over a 15-day period, CHU can identify the count of changes at higher precise levels as compared to calculating changes between new code and original code [14]. The study also suggested 4 decay function types of CHU including WCHU, LDCHU, EDCHU, and LGDCHU. Code Entropy (HH) calculates the number of associated files concerning changes in specific code parameters. Similar to CHU, 4 types of HH are used (HWH, LDHH, EDHH, and LGDHH).

Experimental results of the study suggest that WCHU and LDHH parameters have higher estimation levels overall programs used [36]. However, the model faced shortcoming of the high requirement of resources and information due to the inherent feature of extracting data on a 15-day period from repositories.

5) Popularity parameters: popularity metrics are suggested in [8], focusing on e-mail archives of programmers in a group. The underlying concept of such popularity metrics is that the higher a particular program is communicated in emails, the higher the fault-proneness of the program. Table 2.4 depicts the six popularity parameters discussed in the study. Most of the parameters are for counting the occurrence of the specific class in the email communications. The concept of obtaining parameters from the email discussions is a new approach but the approach faced tough challenges in terms of performance as the model could not outperform other code parameters.

Table 2.4: Popularity metrics [8]

Name	Description
POP-NOM	The number of mails discussing a class
POP-NOCM	The number of characters in all mail discussing a class

POP-NOT	The number of e-mail threads discussing different topics for a class
POP-NOMT	The number of e-mails in a thread discussing a class in at least one of mails in a thread
POP-NOA	The number of authors motioning about the same class

6) Ownership and Programmer Expertise parameters: Four ownership parameters are suggested in [9] based on program authorship. Ownership is the extent of commitment to the program and is defined as greater than or less than 5%. The contribution of over 5% is considered majority ownership and lower than 5% is considered as minority ownership. Four parameters discussed in the study include MINOR, MAJOR, TOTAL, and OWNERSHIP. The study depicted that the greater the ownership, the lesser the chances of fault occurrence. In [37], a further in-depth analysis of faults and ownership or author expertise is conducted. An attractive outcome of the research is that for achieving minimal faults, the source code must be developed by high expertise programmers and the contribution of fewer expertise authors should be minimal.

7) MIM parameters: Micro interaction parameters (MIM) obtained from Mylyn are used for fault estimation in [12]. These parameters compute the number of author interactions with Eclipse. The basic concept of MIM is that author' mistakes determine the number of faults. For instance, multiple editing of code can lead to higher fault-proneness. A total of 56 parameters are obtained from Mylyn study and are evaluated on their efficiency in fault proneness as compared to code parameters and process parameters. Study results show superior performance of MIM parameters compared to other code and process parameters. However, use of MIM parameters to different applications is limited as all of them can not support Mylyn.

2.2.3 Other Parameters

In addition to code and process parameters, several other types of parameters relying on available approaches are suggested in [38], [39], [35], [40].

In [38], researchers obtained developer parameters from a social networking platform to depict collaboration framework obtained from version systems or archives. From this platform, researchers observed a strong correlation between program faults and developer network parameters.

The study in [39] also relied on developer network concept but extended to include developer contribution network. Estimation accuracy is found to be greatly improved by incorporating the new concept.

Data dependency graphs of binaries are used in [35]. The researchers conducted extensive network analysis over these graphs and identified new parameters of proximity, betweenness etc. Estimation models are developed and upon comparison with code and process parameters, the suggested parameters depicted higher efficiency.

The study in [40] developed 4 anti-pattern parameters, which are loose program designs allowing fault flows smoothly in the corresponding codes. Anti-pattern parameters also posed higher efficiency as compared to code and process parameters.

2.2.4 Comparison of Code parameters with Process parameters

Figure 2.2 depicts the number of times a particular parameter was incorporated in related fault estimation studies in the literature. As code parameters have been in use from the early 1990s, they are used more times compared to other parameters. Further, several code parameter comparison studies were conducted as and when a new parameter was suggested. On the contrary, process parameters have been studies from the 2000s, with the emergence of storage concepts like program archives in CVS systems.

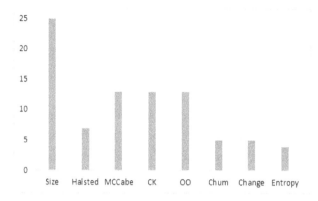

Figure 2.2: Use frequency of defect prediction metrics in the representative defect prediction papers

Despite the availability of multiple types of parameters, the importance of code parameters continues to exist. These parameters are relevant in current conditions for constructing fault estimation tools [13]. However, [41] suggests that the code parameters have low performance compared to process parameters due to their stagnant nature.

2.3 Fault Estimation Models

Most fault estimation approaches are being developed through the concept of machine learning. Based on the required outcome such as proneness of bug count, these approached are categorized as classifiers and regression-based. With increasing prominence of machine learning approaches, both supervised and partially-supervised approaches are being present to accurately estimate fault proneness [42], [43]. In addition, other approaches like BugCache are also suggested [44].

Figure 2.3 depicts the number of times that different fault estimation approaches have been studied in the contemporary literature. Similar to code parameters, as statistical approaches incorporating machine learning techniques are used for longer periods, these approaches remain largest in terms of frequency. As suggested in [44], few researchers also studied the efficiency of other approaches like BugCache [45], [46], [47].

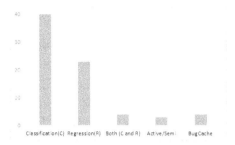

Figure 2.3: Use frequency of defect prediction models in the representative defect prediction papers.

Both the categories of machine learning opt for same estimation procedure. Both the models differ in the aspect of estimation requirement. While classification approach is typically deployed for detecting susceptibility to bugs, regression approach estimates the count of bugs [13], [29], [48], [14], [49], [35]. The choice of approach varies with the requirement of programmers or end-users. Figure 2.4 details the number of times a particular approach has been studied in the contemporary literature. Evaluation is done mostly on the basis of logistic regression in addition to NB algorithm and Decision Tree approaches.

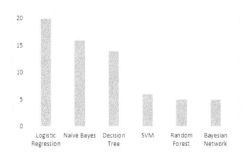

Figure 2.4: Use frequency of classification machine learners in the representative defect prediction papers.

Similar to classification approach, regression approach also has been evaluated with linear regression. In addition, negative binomial regression techniques were also implemented [9], [10], [4], [12], [50], [51], [52]. Technological advances in machine learning approach with full or partial supervised models, an increasing number of researchers continue to deploy these techniques for fault estimation.

2.4 Preprocessing Strategies

Preprocessing strategies form the vital part of successful implementation of machine learning approaches. Several researchers focused on developing efficient strategies for fault estimation through machine learning models [15], [13], [16], [17], [18]. However, the usability of these strategies and selection of the right strategy is dependent on multiple parameters including the type of approach, involved subjects etc.

2.4.1 Normalization

Normalization strategy involves assigning weights to selected parameters, thereby, leading to classification approach performance enhancement [53], [54].

2.4.2 Feature selection and extraction

Feature selection algorithm (FSA) is a computational model, which is motivated by specific description of significance. An experimental comparison of dissimilar feature selection algorithms has been presented by L. Ladha. In universal, the feature selection is described as a search difficult according to some evaluation criteria. Feature selection algorithms can categorize by (a) search association: exponential, random, and possible sequential are the three kinds of search (b) Generation of successors (subset): Forward, Backward, Compound, Weighted, and Random these are five dissimilar operators can be considered to create the successor. (c) Evaluation Measure: evaluation of beneficiaries can be measure through Interclass Distance, Probability of Error, Dependence, Deviation, Information or Uncertainty and Reliability Evaluation.

Feature selection approaches are distinguished into three groups: Wrappers, Filters, and Embedded/Hybrid Method. Filter approaches have low computational charge and faster however, with incompetent consistency in classification as compared to wrapper methods and improved suitable for high dimensional data sets. Filter approaches can divide into two types, specifically, feature weighting algorithms and subset search algorithms. Feature weighting algorithms allocate weights to features separately and rank them based on their significance to the target approach. Wrapper approaches perform better than filter approaches because feature selection procedure is enhanced for the classifier to be used but wrapper approaches have expensive to be used for huge feature space because of high computational charge and every feature set should be estimated with the qualified classifier, which eventually make feature selection process slow. Hybrid/ Embedded approaches are newly improved that utilize benefits of both wrapper and filter methods. A hybrid method utilizes both an independent test and presentation estimation function of the feature subset.

Feature Extraction/Transformation

Feature extraction attains some transformation of original features to create additional features, which are more important. Feature extraction can be utilized in this condition to decrease difficulty and give a simple design of data signifying each variable in feature space as a linear mixture of the original input variable. Principle Component Analysis (PCA) is the most common and broadly used feature extraction method.

2.4.3 Noise control

To reduce bias in data extracted from CVS systems and storage repositories, noise detection and control strategies are proposed in [55]. The key reason for this noise is due to automated extraction of fault data by algorithms [56], [57].

3

Software Error Estimation Models Proposed In Literature

3.1 Conventional Models for Fault Estimation

Conventional approaches in contemporary literature can group into the following categories-

- Human Expert Insights Based
- Analogy-Based
- Regression-Based

Statistical models using regression analysis are also studied in the literature for fault estimation. The resultant variable is generally classified as faulty or non-faulty similar to simple regression technique. Alternatively, the resultant can be the count of anticipated faults similar to multiple regression techniques. The studies in [58] and [59] incorporated simple linear regression analysis for detecting fault-proneness of the program. The study in [60] deployed multiple regression analysis using program modifications as the primary input parameter. Researchers in [61] also used linear regression technique for estimating errors in two subsystems of an OS. Further, least square regression, MRE error etc. are also utilized in the study.

3.2 Machine Learning Models for Fault Estimation

Machine learning (ML) approaches are increasingly being studied for fault estimation of a code driven by their superior performance in accurately detecting fault-proneness. Code parameters obtained from NASA IV & V MDP along with NB algorithm are studied in [13]. The model resulted in 71% accuracy rates with a False alarm Rate (pf) of 25%. NASA JM1 data is analyzed in [62] with the accuracy of fault estimation rate of 72.6% accuracy using ANNs and using SVMs, it achieved 87.4% accuracy rates.

The study in [63] analyzed data gathered from 31 different program codes. IT used BNNs to achieve R2 of 0.93 between parameters of estimated faults and actual faults. In [2], researchers evaluated multiple feature subsets and suggested that implementing ML techniques for fault estimation is practical and feasible at low costs.

Based on the results and suggestions of the aforementioned research works, we can conclude that most of the studies compare different ML approaches in terms of accuracy of estimation. However, these studies have limited or no focus on different dimensions for comparison.

Further, studies focusing on technology also successfully depicted that including complex techniques varies with different factors [64], [65]. Based on the TRA theory [66], the study in [67] constructed TAM model to illustrate developer acceptance of system generated data. The TAM model was implemented in multiple research works to detail acceptance of system technologies like OOPs by programmers [68], gender dissimilarities in understanding email use [69], Internet-based information use [70].

The study in [64] utilized adaption structure suggested in [71] to successfully depict factors affecting acceptance of open systems in the business environment. The results suggest higher acceptance levels in organizations driven by their ability to adapt the model rather than model advantages. In addition, the study also observed that most organizations tend to show reactive attitude instead of a proactive approach. In [65], the researchers utilized TAM model to advocate support for the model acceptance in estimating program measures.

This manuscript adapts TAM model and framework proposed in [71] to identify the most significant factors for evaluating the use of ML techniques for fault estimation analysis [72]. Further, this research work also presents the organizational acceptance to the factors and associated attributes. The organization acceptance remains vital as it enables the researcher to gain meaningful insights into the required outcomes. Framework and extent of knowledge on attribute significance provide the required scope of future studies incorporating machine learning tools for attribute comparison.

4

Features Selection Strategies

4.1 Choosing Relevant Features

Detecting all relevant features and selecting the right one is the crucial preprocessing stage of a data mining technique in addition to deleting unnecessary features. The current feature selection techniques can classify into two broad segments- on the basis of the filter and on the basis of the wrapper. The former set of methods relies on essential features of a database and these techniques are given ranks [73]. Accordingly, the filter based techniques do not incorporate ML algorithms. On the other hand, methods using wrappers compare the features on their significance levels concerning fault estimation accuracy of ML algorithm. As can be observed, the recent techniques involve low overheads compared to the later set of methods. However, the performance of filter based approaches cannot be assured while wrapper based approaches pose higher fault estimation accuracy rates.

4.2 Existing Feature Selection Approaches

SBSE engineering approaches are being increasingly implemented in addressing optimization tasks such as planning, upgrading, and re-coding works. In [74] and [75], researchers developed a detailed analysis of SBSE based papers. In our research work, we propose unique insights on choosing optimal features for fault estimation methods.

In [76] and [77], features were chosen based on 3 filtering methods and 3 wrapper methods. The techniques were applied to five databases. The study results suggest that reduced databases had same estimation accuracy despite the reduction in the number of attributes. Further, the study depicted that wrapper methods had higher accuracy rates compared to filter methods but the costs involved in the above process are higher than the following method. However, these outcomes are based on the comparison based on cross-validation and not independent database. As can be understood, the performance of an approach can be considered high only if it can be generalized and not on cross-validations. Generalization becomes essential because it exposes models specifically tailored to the training database. Accordingly, our paper incorporates three different and independent datasets to ensure generalization of the model. The study in [78] evaluated wrapper model regarding overheads involved and resource requirement. The study also confirmed that reduced databases lead to boost prediction rates.

In [79], researchers surveyed available feature detection strategies and provided a comprehensive analysis of feature selection process. In [80], significant proposes for optimal attribute detection such as feature building, ranking, multivariate, validation and search processes. In [73], 6 selection approaches based on feature ranking are compared over 15 databases in UCI repository. The study observed that feature ranking resulted in similar performances, wrapper/filter methods were better for choosing optimal features.

The concept of choosing optimal features has been studied extensively in the context of different application areas [81], [82], [83]. The SVM machine based selection process was considered in [84] and in [85], by evaluating user qualification for feature selection. The study in [82] focused on text mining, where features are assigned either zero or one. The researcher studied the feasibility of applying different filter ranking techniques.

Despite several studies being proposed in the literature, none of the studies compared efficiency of different approached for fault prediction using identified features in the reduced database with all features in the original database. A key reason for lack of this comparison can be restrictions posed by individual domains. For instance, in a dataset with a large number of total features, constructing models incorporating all features is complex and thereby, restricting further comparison. Further, feature patterns of specific datasets cannot extend to other applications. For example, binary features found in text mining may not be observed in other applications. In our research work, we considered features with numbers in software engineering application. To evaluate the performance of feature selection approaches, models developed with chosen features on reduced databases are compared with features in original databases.

5

Overcoming Shortcomings
of Biased Datasets

Imbalanced or biased data remains one of the prominent issues of data mining programmers, in particular in classification tasks. This is due to high sample volume for some classes and low volume for others. This leads in mining programmers to develop inefficient approaches as the tools often aim for achieving overall high accuracy rates, resulting in the tools posing poor performance in classes with low sample count.

Software Engineering data in general and defect prediction datasets are not an exception, and in this paper, we compare different approaches including data sampling, overheads, machine learning or hybrid learning approaches. For comparison, NASA databases curated by Shepperd are considered. Contrary to most of the available studies, we delete all data duplicates in the pre-processing phase.

5.1 Prologue

Several public databases are observed to be biased towards classes with more samples. Accordingly, most mining programs result in poor performance when dealing with classes with fewer samples as they aim to achieve overall high performance. For instance, in case of non-faulty class samples to faulty class samples ratio is 95%, the model always presumes that classifying the dataset as non-faulty will result in high accuracy rates. Accordingly, most of the mining programs generate imbalanced methods, which ignore the class with low samples.

Ignoring the data bias issue in a dataset can result in ML programs constructing poor models in particular, where specific factors are not an exact or misguiding amount of accuracy rate. This is because, these algorithms, by default, presume the database to balance regarding samples. Biased data issues are also observed in ML programs including decision trees, NNs and SVMs [86]. In these programs, multiple solutions including data sampling, bootstrapping or wrapping different classifiers are practiced to ensure data fed into the model is unbiased.

In our research study, multiple algorithms are evaluated in their efficiency to handle biased data in the context of fault estimation over NASA databases. For this purpose, we consider various comparison parameters including Matthew's Correlation coefficient along with multiple cleaning procedures aimed at deleting repetitions.

5.2 Strategies for handling Biased Datasets

Several approaches have suggested for handling biased data in ML algorithms though none of them has implemented in fault estimation applications. Some of these approaches include data sampling, overhead based, ensemble or hybrid techniques. The prominent methods are discussed in the sections below-

5.2.1 Data Sampling Techniques

Data sampling approaches are incorporated in the pre-processing phase and are categorized into two groups based on adding new samples to minority class or deleting existing samples from majority class. Accordingly, these are classified as either over-sampling or under-sampling respectively. Adding duplicates in samples is termed Random over-sampling (ROS). On the other hand, deletion of duplicates is termed Random Under-Sampling (RUS).

However, advances in the area have resulted in advanced techniques of adding artificial samples to minority class as compared to simple random duplication. On such prominent approach is suggested in [87] and is referred as SMOTE technique. The technique generates samples on the basis of nearby classes. In [88], ENN and Wilson's editing techniques are proposed where ENN selects the neighbors while the editing technique excludes neighboring samples of the different class.

5.2.2 Cost-Sensitive classification (CSC) Techniques

CSC techniques incorporate classifiers to modify biased databases by allocating weights to samples (provided if program permits) or regenerating samples based on costs involved. Alternatively, the CSC technique involves building the new model which can minimize computation overheads (calculated as the product of estimated probability distribution and wrong classification overheads). Though such techniques are used in the theoretical sense, on a practical basis, no organized process of determining the costs is designed. Accordingly, this cost is often assumed same as the costs involved in class distribution.

5.2.3 Ensemble Techniques

Ensembles based ML techniques often merge different methods to arrive at acceptable estimation accuracy rates. Ensemble techniques are broadly grouped under three categories including bagging technique, stacking technique, and boosting technique. This research work has developed with the use of bagging technique and boosting technology.

Bagging technique [89] is a type of base learning techniques is implemented over different same size databases generated from actual data through bootstrapping process. Estimation procedure in bagging techniques is on the voting concept among independent estimates produced by different databases. As no modifications need to make to the program, bagging technique is relatively easy to incorporate. Further, it also utilizes classifier instability to provide different ensembles have different data, thereby ensuring sustained model performance in all data portions. The technique fails to achieve expected performance with NN classifiers.

Boosting ensemble approaches, on the other hand, create different models which work in coordination to enhance data portions where earlier models had low performance. The technique involves varying weights of data instances incorrectly classified. This enables new learning tools to give more emphasis to such instances. The weighted voting concept is applied to all models in the ensemble. In [90], one of the most prominent boosting approaches is proposed. It allocates same weights first and later based on right or wrong instance classification, the weights are varied.

In [91], a random selection of attributes is incorporated. It employs bagging technique with five components to build decision tree based ensemble. PCA analysis chooses the features by integrating feature subsets utilized with a bootstrapped data subset. However, the technique involved high complexity in understanding the outcome unlike decision trees with relative ease of understanding the process.

5.2.4 Hybrid Techniques

The smote-boost approach aims to minimize imbalance involved in learning process. It enhances the weights assigned to the class with low instances. By incorporating SMOTE technique for every cycle of boosting ensures all learners to additional sampling for minority classes. Further, it enables efficient learning and enhanced decision regions for these classes. Accordingly, employing SMOTE at every cycle of boosting for minority classes in an environment where majority classes have the massive presence, ensures the increased probability of choosing minority classes [92]. The smote-boost procedure is an extension of Ada-Boost M2 concept [93] and is an amalgamation of SMOTE and Boosting techniques. However, SMOTE-Boost technique faces two significant shortcomings. The first limitation is higher complexity levels. As SMOTE should detect the k nearest neighbors and then extrapolate between these neighbors to generate new cases. The second major limitation is the oversampling process used in SMOTE-Boost involved large training periods.

RUS-Boost [94] is also a variety of Ada-Boost.M2 process and is similar to SMOTE-Boost technique. While SMOTE is used in all boosting cycles in SMOTE-Boost technique, RUS-Boost incorporates Random-Under-Sampling (RUS). Incorporation of RUS ensures the above mentioned two major limitations of SMOTE-Boost technique are handled. Unlike SMOTE-Boost, RUS-Boost merely removes majority classes on a random basis. With respect to the second limitation, as RUS generates undersized training databases, it involves low training periods [94]. Both boosting procedure and filtering procedure are observed in both the models through RUS-Boost employs RUS as filter and SMOTE-Boost uses SMOTE.

Another popular hybrid approach is studied in [95], which integrates bagging technique with the cost-sensitive approach. The model uses bagging for re-label training to ensure all instances are allocated to the estimation lowering the anticipated overheads. On the basis of new training data, the model incorporates a classifier on the basis of modified re-labeled data. This ensures programmer to gain the clear understanding of the decision-making process.

6

Research Conclusions, Observations and Future Scope

The chapter discusses challenges observed in Fault estimation tools and various suggestions made by prominent studies to address these challenges. The section also attempts to provide solutions to yet-to-be difficulties resolved in Software Fault Estimation process.

6.1 Role of Fault Information in Software Defect Predictions

To efficiently detect errors in software programs and for effective handling these errors or faults, most large companies gather and monitor the wide set of fault associated parameters. Further, the substantial requirement for different kinds of estimations to handle errors to ensure quality in coding is observed. Survey respondents from two entities have been researched to arrive at the clear understanding of the role of various information necessities.

The Table 6.1 below depicts that information requirements can vary from organization to organization. The difference in requirements is variable on multiple factors including the code development process, testing resources and re-verification process in the organization. At VCG organization in the automobile industry, MBD development model is predominantly used. Simulink1 models, incorporating auto-code generation are used for program development in the company. For the company, classifying error-prone files is not given highest priority while Ericsson with code-centric model assigns the highest priority for fault-prone file classification.

Table 6.1: Comparison of Fault Information Requirements across Companies

Importance of Estimation Needs	VCG (QM)	VCG MetricsTL	Ericsson (QM)	Ericsson MetricsTL
Need for classifying error-prone files	L	H	VH	VH
Anticipated need for errors in the code	H	H	L	VH
Anticipated fault inflows in a project	H	H	L	VH
Delivery readiness/ anticipated latent faults	H	VH	H	VH
Severity classification of Faults	VH	M	H	H

As can be observed from the Table 6.1, evaluating delivery readiness is H (high) for VCG and Ericsson with respect to severity fault classification. However, information needs are observed to vary based on their testing and quality assessment levels. At VCG, understanding the number of predicted faults or predicted faulty inflows at any given instance is found to be more resourceful for shifting their testing resources to adhere to expected quality demand. Ericsson, on the other hand, assigns more priority in detecting small file sets prone to errors to assist testing and quality assessment with minimum resources.

6.2 Importance of Attributes in Fault Estimation

Most studies face difficulties in generalizing feature subsets, which play a vital role in classifying module as fault-prone or non-fault prone. Further, multiple opinions are suggested on the parameter level, requirement parameters, design parameters or coding parameters. Multiple studies are suggested in [96], [97], [98], [13], [99] but with different feature subsets proposed. A brief discussion of these studies aimed at handling these feature selection techniques is detailed in the following paragraphs.

In [97], researchers evaluated the importance of design parameter subset in assessing bug proneness and observed it to be the active determinant. OO features also have been incorporated by the researchers. The study outcomes suggest that both inheritance and EC have the strong correlation with error-proneness.

In [99] also, researchers conducted similar model evaluating the importance of method level and class level parameters in estimating error-proneness of files in NASA databases [100]. In [101], decision tree and instance relying on classification models are studied over WEKA to construct fault estimation models. Both the approaches are assessed through precision metrics, recall metrics, and F-measure. Experiment outcomes suggest that big components have superior performance over small components for error estimation. Further, class level parameters are proposed in case of small modules for error estimation.

In [96], the study evaluated if features available with coding developers can assist them in early detection of faults in software development process. Accordingly, these researchers did the comparative analysis of various error estimation models based on different parameters including requirement parameters, code parameters, and combined parameters. Multiple ML algorithms have been deployed including NB algorithm, voted perceptron, linear regression and random forests among others. Outcomes recorded the combination of text parameters with static code parameters have strong estimation accuracy excluding when evaluated using voted perceptron.

In [98], researchers compared different requirement parameters on a quantitative basis with code parameters and the combination of code and requirement parameters. Initially, k-means clustering techniques are implemented during transformation stage, and later, decision tree based ML algorithm is used over MDP data repository [100]. The model recorded 100% precision rates and recall. Accordingly, the model is observed to be applicable in fault estimation tools where parameters are available in early coding stages.

In [13], a different approach has been suggested. The study suggests that building classification models should give high priority over parameters. Eight databases of MDP [100] are used for conducting experiments on the models based on ML algorithms including decision trees, NBs and rile based algorithms. Further, it also analyzed changes in outcomes with and without log filter. Outcomes are evaluated on the basis of recall, balance and low false alarm rates. Experimental results depicted that NB algorithm with log filter has superior performance over other models. This combination is observed to achieve an average Pd of 71% and Pf of 25%.

Analyzing the above models depicts that any of the studies have not established a generalized relation of features with defect prediction.

6.3 Inconsistency in Performance Assessment Methods

Lack of approved standards for measuring error prediction model performance is one of the tough challenges in developing reliable models. Wide inconsistency exists among recording model performance across multiple applications and studies. Studies focusing on performance assessment by popular studies are depicted in the following paragraphs.

In [13], authors suggested recall and Pf for model performance assessment. Comparing it with precision, the author depicted the issue of precision instability and accordingly proposed that it can avoid from usage in the operational evaluation.

The study in [102] advocated for the use of cross-project error estimation must engage precision despite bias issues in data (discussed in section 6.7). 13 datasets extracted from MDP repository are utilized for evaluations. Multiple classification approaches are compared based on recall, false alarm probability, and precision. The study concluded that precision should include the biased class task.

In [103], the research work focused on the importance of variance for comparing different error estimation models. Method resulting in the least variance levels is found to have better performance. Through statistical analysis of 12 datasets of MDP, the role of the variance in performance evaluation is observed. Recall, precision and F-measure and AUC are considered as selection criteria and deployed Random Forest, NB algorithm, Boosting and Bagging techniques.

Experimental results suggest the AUC possesses small variance and it is accordingly considered as relatively static.

Though the above studies proposed the use of report call along with other selection criteria but failed to arrive at the standard set of criteria.

6.4 Cross-Project Fault Estimation Challenges

Models learning from locally existing information are highly preferred because of local data similarity with test data. The local information can obtain from earlier versions of the same code or can also obtain from similar coding developed through the same language. However, often the local information is not readily available for the risk mitigation manager of a company. This lack of training data can spur from multiple factors including non-availability of the similar project in the company or advances in technology.

Accordingly, most of the current literature is being focused on cross-project information for fault estimation. However, strong future scope exists regarding improvising models based on this area.

6.5 Lack of Standard Framework

One of the other key challenges affiliated with fault prediction models is different studies relying on different databases. Lack of general procedure for fault prediction models remains tough challenges for both local data based and cross-project based research. Some researchers attempted to use multiple frameworks for incorporating fault estimation models. Of these, two research works [23], [104] are advantageous, but both the approaches are not generalized and vary largely with each other.

6.6 Costs Involved in Software Fault Estimation Models

Despite several studies being developed focusing on the relative ease of implementing fault estimation models, only some studies considered the cost dynamics of the implementation process. Misclassification can involve enormous costs for the organization, in particular, when classifying the component as defect prone or not. Accordingly, there arises the strong need for addressing the instance and extent of a utility gains prominence. Only a few studies focused on this aspect and [105], [106] are observed to be popular studies. Both the studies focused on cost dynamics of the fault prediction model, but the area offers large research scope.

6.7 Biased Class Information Challenge

Accuracy in class-distribution of training datasets holds the key to the successful functioning of a fault estimation model [107]. Class-distribution is defined as the count of instances of all classes in the database. Higher instances of single class superseding other class instance count can lead to faulty prediction, and this problem is termed as a biased class issue or imbalance problem [108]. Classes with higher instances are considered as majority classes, and the classes with fewer instances are termed minority classes. In particular, when the faulty class has fewer instances and falls under minority class category, fault prediction model developers face much tough challenges.

However, several studies attempted to address the biased class problem, but the overall performance of almost all studies is observed to be similar. This leads to ambiguity to continue as no single technique is considered as the final solution to handle class imbalance issue.

6.8 Machine Learning Approach Issues in Fault Prediction

In addition to general challenges discussed in earlier sections, the following paragraphs detail issues specific to deploying machine learning approaches for fault estimation models. These are real-time queries often faced by industry professionals.

Time constraints and Efficiency need for risk reduction - As companies often announce delivery times long before project commencement, time periods involved in testing remains key for quality delivery and on-time launch. Accordingly, adaptability of ML approaches in an industrial environment for fault prediction is largely based on the times involved. Further, risk reduction efficiency also serves as an attractive feature for companies to implement ML techniques.

Limited or no access to original code- As companies also procure software from external sources apart from internal sources, source code and modification parameters may not be accessible. This puts the implementation of ML approaches in such environment under uncertainty and can be ineffective in defect prediction.

Implementing machine learning for model-driven development concept- The concept is increasingly observed in multiple domains including aviation industry and automobile industry. Adapting ML approaches to cater requirements of these industries still remains unanswered.

The extent of applicability of ML techniques to analyze prediction accuracy- The question of can ML techniques be extended to error prediction in cases like Simulink continues to remain. Further, if the accuracy of parameters auto-generated from ML technique based models is suitable for SDP also needed to be addressed.

Effective utilization of text artifacts for fault prediction: As most ML techniques for fault prediction depend on quantitative information, extending the techniques for environments comprising text-based artifacts is to be demonstrated. The capability of ML approaches to process text-based information will increase the adaptability of these techniques in the industrial environment.

Continued ambiguity on the ML approaches to adhere to standards: Industries like automobile domain prefer strict adherence to safety standards, emphasizing on incorporating formal approaches for program verification. Adaptability of ML approaches to fit in this context and its capability of guaranteeing adherence to strict standards, which needs to be further explored.

REFERENCES

1. Seliya, Naeem, Taghi M. Khoshgoftaar, and Jason Van Hulse. "Predicting faults in high assurance software." High-Assurance Systems Engineering (HASE), 2010 IEEE 12th International Symposium on. IEEE, 2010.

2. Menzies, Tim, et al. "How simple is software defect detection." Submitted to the Empirical Software Engineering Journal (2003).

3. Legris, Paul, John Ingham, and Pierre Collerette. "Why do people use information technology? A critical review of the technology acceptance model." Information & management 40.3 (2003): 191-204.

4. Kamei, Yasutaka, et al. "Revisiting common bug prediction findings using effort-aware models." Software Maintenance (ICSM), 2010 IEEE International Conference on. IEEE, 2010.

5. Nagappan, Nachiappan, Thomas Ball, and Andreas Zeller. "Mining metrics to predict component failures." Proceedings of the 28th international conference on Software engineering. ACM, 2006.

6. Zhang, Hongyu, Xiuzhen Zhang, and Ming Gu. "Predicting defective software components from code complexity measures." Dependable Computing, 2007. PRDC 2007. 13th Pacific Rim International Symposium on. IEEE, 2007.

7. Kim, Sunghun, et al. "Automatic identification of bug-introducing changes." Automated Software Engineering,

2006. ASE'06. 21st IEEE/ACM International Conference on. IEEE, 2006.

8.   Bacchelli, Alberto, Marco D'Ambros, and Michele Lanza. "Are popular classes more defect prone?." International Conference on Fundamental Approaches to Software Engineering. Springer, Berlin, Heidelberg, 2010.

9.   Bird, Christian, et al. "Don't touch my code!: examining the effects of ownership on software quality." Proceedings of the 19th ACM SIGSOFT symposium and the 13th European conference on Foundations of software engineering. ACM, 2011.

10.   D'Ambros, Marco, Michele Lanza, and Romain Robbes. "Evaluating defect prediction approaches: a benchmark and an extensive comparison." Empirical Software Engineering 17.4-5 (2012): 531-577.

11.   Hassan, Ahmed E. "Predicting faults using the complexity of code changes." Proceedings of the 31st International Conference on Software Engineering. IEEE Computer Society, 2009.

12.   Lee, Taek, et al. "Micro interaction metrics for defect prediction." Proceedings of the 19th ACM SIGSOFT symposium and the 13th European conference on Foundations of software engineering. ACM, 2011.

13.   Menzies, Tim, Jeremy Greenwald, and Art Frank. "Data mining static code attributes to learn defect predictors." IEEE transactions on software engineering 33.1 (2007): 2-13.

14.   Nagappan, Nachiappan, and Thomas Ball. "Use of relative code churn measures to predict system defect density." Software Engineering, 2005. ICSE 2005. Proceedings. 27th International Conference on. IEEE, 2005.

15.   Kim, Sunghun, et al. "Dealing with noise in defect prediction." Software Engineering (ICSE), 2011 33rd International Conference on. IEEE, 2011.

16.   Nam, Jaechang, Sinno Jialin Pan, and Sunghun Kim. "Transfer defect learning." Proceedings of the 2013 International Conference on Software Engineering. IEEE Press, 2013.

17. Shivaji, Shivkumar, et al. "Reducing features to improve code change-based bug prediction." IEEE Transactions on Software Engineering 39.4 (2013): 552-569.

18. Wu, Rongxin, et al. "Relink: recovering links between bugs and changes." Proceedings of the 19th ACM SIGSOFT symposium and the 13th European conference on Foundations of software engineering. ACM, 2011.

19. Conte, Samuel Daniel, Hubert E. Dunsmore, and Vincent Y. Shen. Software engineering metrics and models. Benjamin-Cummings Publishing Co., Inc., 1986.

20. Akiyama, Fumio. "An Example of Software System Debugging." IFIP Congress (1). Vol. 71. 1971.

21. Hata, Hideaki, Osamu Mizuno, and Tohru Kikuno. "Bug prediction based on fine-grained module histories." Proceedings of the 34th International Conference on Software Engineering. IEEE Press, 2012.

22. Shihab, Emad, et al. "High-impact defects: a study of breakage and surprise defects." Proceedings of the 19th ACM SIGSOFT symposium and the 13th European conference on Foundations of software engineering. ACM, 2011.

23. Song, Qinbao, et al. "A general software defect-proneness prediction framework." IEEE Transactions on Software Engineering 37.3 (2011): 356-370.

24. Halstead, Maurice Howard. Elements of software science. Vol. 7. New York: Elsevier, 1977.

25. Turhan, Burak, et al. "On the relative value of cross-company and within-company data for defect prediction." Empirical Software Engineering 14.5 (2009): 540-578.

26. McCabe, Thomas J. "A complexity measure." IEEE Transactions on software Engineering 4 (1976): 308-320.

27. Ohlsson, Niclas, and Hans Alberg. "Predicting fault-prone software modules in telephone switches." IEEE Transactions on Software Engineering 22.12 (1996): 886-894.

28. Lessmann, Stefan, et al. "Benchmarking classification models for software defect prediction: A proposed framework and

novel findings." IEEE Transactions on Software Engineering 34.4 (2008): 485-496.

29. Moser, Raimund, Witold Pedrycz, and Giancarlo Succi. "A comparative analysis of the efficiency of change metrics and static code attributes for defect prediction." Proceedings of the 30th international conference on Software engineering. ACM, 2008.

30. Chidamber, Shyam R., and Chris F. Kemerer. "A metrics suite for object oriented design." IEEE Transactions on software engineering 20.6 (1994): 476-493.

31. Basili, Victor R., Lionel C. Briand, and Walcélio L. Melo. "A validation of object-oriented design metrics as quality indicators." IEEE Transactions on software engineering 22.10 (1996): 751-761.

32. Pai, Ganesh J., and Joanne Bechta Dugan. "Empirical analysis of software fault content and fault proneness using Bayesian methods." IEEE Transactions on software Engineering 33.10 (2007).

33. e Abreu, Fernando Brito, and Rogério Carapuça. "Candidate metrics for object-oriented software within a taxonomy framework." Journal of Systems and Software 26.1 (1994): 87-96.

34. Zhang, Hongyu, and Rongxin Wu. "Sampling program quality." Software Maintenance (ICSM), 2010 IEEE International Conference on. IEEE, 2010.

35. Zimmermann, Thomas, and Nachiappan Nagappan. "Predicting defects using network analysis on dependency graphs." Software Engineering, 2008. ICSE'08. ACM/IEEE 30th International Conference on. IEEE, 2008.

36. D'Ambros, Marco, Michele Lanza, and Romain Robbes. "An extensive comparison of bug prediction approaches." Mining Software Repositories (MSR), 2010 7th IEEE Working Conference on. IEEE, 2010.

37. Rahman, Foyzur, and Premkumar Devanbu. "Ownership, experience and defects: a fine-grained study of authorship."

Proceedings of the 33rd International Conference on Software Engineering. ACM, 2011.

38. Meneely, Andrew, et al. "Predicting failures with developer networks and social network analysis." Proceedings of the 16th ACM SIGSOFT International Symposium on Foundations of software engineering. ACM, 2008.

39. Pinzger, Martin, Nachiappan Nagappan, and Brendan Murphy. "Can developer-module networks predict failures?." Proceedings of the 16th ACM SIGSOFT International Symposium on Foundations of software engineering. ACM, 2008.

40. Taba, Seyyed Ehsan Salamati, et al. "Predicting bugs using anti-patterns." Software Maintenance (ICSM), 2013 29th IEEE International Conference on. IEEE, 2013.

41. Rahman, Foyzur, and Premkumar Devanbu. "How, and why, process metrics are better." Proceedings of the 2013 International Conference on Software Engineering. IEEE Press, 2013.

42. Li, Ming, et al. "Sample-based software defect prediction with active and semi-supervised learning." Automated Software Engineering 19.2 (2012): 201-230.

43. Lu, Huihua, and Bojan Cukic. "An adaptive approach with active learning in software fault prediction." Proceedings of the 8th International Conference on Predictive Models in Software Engineering. ACM, 2012.

44. Kim, Sunghun, et al. "Predicting faults from cached history." Proceedings of the 29th international conference on Software Engineering. IEEE Computer Society, 2007.

45. Engström, Emelie, Per Runeson, and Greger Wikstrand. "An empirical evaluation of regression testing based on fix-cache recommendations." Software Testing, Verification and Validation (ICST), 2010 Third International Conference on. IEEE, 2010.

46. Lewis, Chris, et al. "Does bug prediction support human developers? findings from a Google case study." Proceedings of

39

the 2013 International Conference on Software Engineering. IEEE Press, 2013.

47. Rahman, Foyzur, et al. "Bug Cache for inspections: hit or miss?." Proceedings of the 19th ACM SIGSOFT symposium and the 13th European conference on Foundations of software engineering. ACM, 2011.

48. Zimmermann, Thomas, et al. "Cross-project defect prediction: a large scale experiment on data vs. domain vs. process." Proceedings of the 7th joint meeting of the European software engineering conference and the ACM SIGSOFT symposium on the foundations of software engineering. ACM, 2009.

49. Nagappan, Nachiappan, and Thomas Ball. "Static analysis tools as early indicators of pre-release defect density." Proceedings of the 27th international conference on Software engineering. ACM, 2005.

50. Ostrand, Thomas J., Elaine J. Weyuker, and Robert M. Bell. "Predicting the location and number of faults in large software systems." IEEE Transactions on Software Engineering 31.4 (2005): 340-355.

51. Shin, Yonghee, et al. "Evaluating complexity, code churn, and developer activity metrics as indicators of software vulnerabilities." IEEE Transactions on Software Engineering 37.6 (2011): 772-787.

52. Weyuker, Elaine J., Thomas J. Ostrand, and Robert M. Bell. "Comparing the effectiveness of several modeling methods for fault prediction." Empirical Software Engineering 15.3 (2010): 277-295.

53. Han, Jiawei, Jian Pei, and Micheline Kamber. Data mining: concepts and techniques. Elsevier, 2011.

54. Graf, Arnulf BA, and Silvio Borer. "Normalization in support vector machines." Pattern Recognition: 23rd DAGM Symposium, Munich, Germany, September 12-14, 2001. Proceedings. Springer Berlin/Heidelberg, 2001.

55. Bird, Christian, et al. "Fair and balanced?: bias in bug-fix datasets." Proceedings of the the 7th joint meeting of the

European software engineering conference and the ACM SIGSOFT symposium on The foundations of software engineering. ACM, 2009.

56. Aversano, Lerina, Luigi Cerulo, and Concettina Del Grosso. "Learning from bug-introducing changes to prevent fault prone code." Ninth international workshop on Principles of software evolution: in conjunction with the 6th ESEC/FSE joint meeting. ACM, 2007.

57. Śliwerski, Jacek, Thomas Zimmermann, and Andreas Zeller. «When do changes induce fixes?.» ACM sigsoft software engineering notes. Vol. 30. No. 4. ACM, 2005.

58. Khoshgoftaar, Taghi M., and Edward B. Allen. "Logistic regression modeling of software quality." International Journal of Reliability, Quality and Safety Engineering 6.04 (1999): 303-317.

59. Zimmermann, Thomas, Rahul Premraj, and Andreas Zeller. "Predicting defects for eclipse." Proceedings of the third international workshop on predictor models in software engineering. IEEE Computer Society, 2007.

60. Khoshgoftaar, Taghi M., John C. Munson, and David L. Lanning. "A comparative study of predictive models for program changes during system testing and maintenance." Software Maintenance, 1993. CSM-93, Proceedings., Conference on. IEEE, 1993.

61. Khoshgoftaar, Taghi M., et al. "Predictive modeling techniques of software quality from software measures." IEEE Transactions on Software Engineering 18.11 (1992): 979-987.

62. Gondra, Iker. "Applying machine learning to software fault-proneness prediction." Journal of Systems and Software 81.2 (2008): 186-195.

63. Fenton, Norman, et al. "On the effectiveness of early life cycle defect prediction with Bayesian Nets." Empirical Software Engineering 13.5 (2008): 499.

64. Chau, Patrick YK, and Kar Yan Tam. "Factors affecting the adoption of open systems: an exploratory study." MIS quarterly (1997): 1-24.

65. Wallace, Linda G., and Steven D. Sheetz. "The adoption of software measures: A technology acceptance model (TAM) perspective." Information & Management 51.2 (2014): 249-259.

66. Ajzen, Icek, and Martin Fishbein. "Understanding attitudes and predicting social behaviour." (1980).

67. Davis, F. D. "A technology acceptance model for empirically testing new end-user information systems: theory and results." (1986).

68. Hardgrave, Bill C., and Richard A. Johnson. "Toward an information systems development acceptance model: the case of object-oriented systems development." IEEE Transactions on Engineering Management 50.3 (2003): 322-336.

69. Gefen, David, and Detmar W. Straub. "Gender differences in the perception and use of e-mail: An extension to the technology acceptance model." MIS quarterly (1997): 389-400.

70. Mun, Y. Yi, and Yujong Hwang. "Predicting the use of web-based information systems: self-efficacy, enjoyment, learning goal orientation, and the technology acceptance model." International journal of human-computer studies 59.4 (2003): 431-449.

71. Tornatzky, Louis G., Mitchell Fleischer, and Alok K. Chakrabarti. Processes of technological innovation. Lexington Books, 1990.

72. Fenton, Norman E., and Martin Neil. "A critique of software defect prediction models." IEEE Transactions on software engineering 25.5 (1999): 675-689.

73. Hall, Mark A., and Geoffrey Holmes. "Benchmarking attribute selection techniques for discrete class data mining." IEEE Transactions on Knowledge and Data engineering 15.6 (2003): 1437-1447.

74. Harman, Mark, S. Afshin Mansouri, and Yuanyuan Zhang. "Search based software engineering: A comprehensive analysis and review of trends techniques and applications." Department of Computer Science, King's College London, Tech. Rep. TR-09-03 (2009).

75. Harman, Mark. "The current state and future of search based software engineering." 2007 Future of Software Engineering. IEEE Computer Society, 2007.

76. Rodríguez, Daniel, et al. "Detecting fault modules applying feature selection to classifiers." Information Reuse and Integration, 2007. IRI 2007. IEEE International Conference on. IEEE, 2007.

77. Rodriguez, Daniel, et al. "Attribute selection in software engineering datasets for detecting fault modules." Software Engineering and Advanced Applications, 2007. 33rd EUROMICRO Conference on. IEEE, 2007.

78. Chen, Zhihao, et al. "Finding the right data for software cost modeling." IEEE software 22.6 (2005): 38-46.

79. Liu, Huan, and Lei Yu. "Toward integrating feature selection algorithms for classification and clustering." IEEE Transactions on knowledge and data engineering 17.4 (2005): 491-502.

80. Guyon, Isabelle, and André Elisseeff. "An introduction to variable and feature selection." Journal of machine learning research 3.Mar (2003): 1157-1182.

81. Furlanello, Cesare, et al. "Entropy-based gene ranking without selection bias for the predictive classification of microarray data." BMC bioinformatics 4.1 (2003): 54.

82. Forman, George. "An extensive empirical study of feature selection metrics for text classification." Journal of machine learning research 3.Mar (2003): 1289-1305.

83. Doraisamy, Shyamala, et al. "A Study on Feature Selection and Classification Techniques for Automatic Genre Classification of Traditional Malay Music." ISMIR. 2008.

84. Jong, Kees, et al. "Feature selection in proteomic pattern data with support vector machines." Computational Intelligence in

Bioinformatics and Computational Biology, 2004. CIBCB'04. Proceedings of the 2004 IEEE Symposium on. IEEE, 2004.

85. Ilczuk, G., et al. "New feature selection methods for qualification of the patients for cardiac pacemaker implantation." Computers in Cardiology, 2007. IEEE, 2007.

86. Japkowicz, Nathalie, and Shaju Stephen. "The class imbalance problem: A systematic study." Intelligent data analysis 6.5 (2002): 429-449.

87. Chawla, Nitesh V., et al. "SMOTE: synthetic minority over-sampling technique." Journal of artificial intelligence research 16 (2002): 321-357.

88. Wilson, Dennis L. "Asymptotic properties of nearest neighbor rules using edited data." IEEE Transactions on Systems, Man, and Cybernetics 2.3 (1972): 408-421.

89. Breiman, Leo. "Bagging predictors." Machine learning 24.2 (1996): 123-140.

90. Freund, Yoav, and Robert E. Schapire. "Experiments with a new boosting algorithm." Icml. Vol. 96. 1996.

91. Rodriguez, Juan José, Ludmila I. Kuncheva, and Carlos J. Alonso. "Rotation forest: A new classifier ensemble method." IEEE transactions on pattern analysis and machine intelligence 28.10 (2006): 1619-1630.

92. Chawla, Nitesh, et al. "SMOTE Boost: Improving prediction of the minority class in boosting." Knowledge Discovery in Databases: PKDD 2003 (2003): 107-119.

93. Freund, Yoav, and Robert E. Schapire. "A Decision-Theoretic Generalization of On-Line Learning and an Application to Boosting." Journal of Computer and System Sciences 55.1 (1997): 119-139.

94. Seiffert, Chris, et al. "RUS Boost: A hybrid approach to alleviating class imbalance." IEEE Transactions on Systems, Man, and Cybernetics-Part A: Systems and Humans 40.1 (2010): 185-197.

95. Domingos, Pedro. "Meta cost: A general method for making classifiers cost-sensitive." Proceedings of the fifth ACM

SIGKDD international conference on Knowledge discovery and data mining. ACM, 1999.

96. Jiang, Yue, Bojan Cukic, and Tim Menzies. "Fault prediction using early lifecycle data." Software Reliability, 2007. ISSRE'07. The 18th IEEE International Symposium on. IEEE, 2007.

97. El Emam, Khaled, Walcelio Melo, and Javam C. Machado. "The prediction of faulty classes using object-oriented design metrics." Journal of Systems and Software 56.1 (2001): 63-75.

98. Sandhu, Parvinder S., et al. "A model for early prediction of faults in software systems." Computer and Automation Engineering (ICCAE), 2010 the 2nd International Conference on. Vol. 4. IEEE, 2010.

99. Koru, A. Gunes, and Hongfang Liu. "Building effective defect-prediction models in practice." IEEE software 22.6 (2005): 23-29.

100. http://mdp.ivv.nasa.gov.

101. http://www.cs.waikato.ac.nz/ml/weka/.

102. Gray, David, et al. "Further thoughts on precision." Evaluation & Assessment in Software Engineering (EASE 2011), 15th Annual Conference on. IET, 2011.

103. Jiang, Yue, et al. "Variance analysis in software fault prediction models." Software Reliability Engineering, 2009. ISSRE'09. 20th International Symposium on. IEEE, 2009.

104. Chen, Ning, Steven CH Hoi, and Xiaokui Xiao. "Software process evaluation: a machine learning framework with application to defect management process." Empirical Software Engineering 19.6 (2014): 1531-1564.

105. Jiang, Yue, Bojan Cukic, and Tim Menzies. "Cost curve evaluation of fault prediction models." Software Reliability Engineering, 2008. ISSRE 2008. 19th International Symposium on. IEEE, 2008.

106. Bathia D, Gupta A. A framework to assess the effectiveness of fault-prediction techniques for quality assurance. In: 7th CSI International Conference on Software Engineering. Punc; 2013. p. 40-49.

107. Batista, Gustavo EAPA, Ronaldo C. Prati, and Maria Carolina Monard. "A study of the behavior of several methods for balancing machine learning training data." ACM Sigkdd Explorations Newsletter 6.1 (2004): 20-29.

108. Galar, Mikel, et al. "A review on ensembles for the class imbalance problem: bagging-, boosting-, and hybrid-based approaches." IEEE Transactions on Systems, Man, and Cybernetics, Part C (Applications and Reviews) 42.4 (2012): 463-484.

1. **KSN PRASAD**

   Kalli Srinivasa Nageswara Prasad is a professor of Computer Science and Engineering Department in GVVR Institute of Technology, Bhimavaram affiliated to Jawaharlal Nehru Technological University, Kakinada, Andhra Pradesh. He received his Ph.D. in Data Mining from Sri Venkateswara University, Tirupathi. He obtained M. Tech degree in Computer Science and Engineering from JNTUK Kakinada, M.S. degree in Software Systems from BITS-Pilani, AMIE in Computer Science and Engineering from Institution of Engineers(India). He has more than 20 years of teaching experience. He has published around 20 research papers in reputed National & International journals and attended many workshops and conferences. Many of the students have guided in their projects & thesis. His research interests are Data Mining & Big Data. He is a life member of ISTE & IEI.

2. **ANNALURI SREENIVASA RAO**

   Annaluri Sreenivasa Rao is having 20 years of Teaching experience. He participated in various Conferences, Seminars, Workshops and published 17 papers in reputed Journals and Conferences. Presently working as an Assistant Professor in the department of Computer Science and Engineering at VNR Vignana Jyothi Institute of Engineering and Technology, Hyderabad. He has a Membership with Computer Society of India and ISTE. His areas of interest is Data mining and Machine learning.

3. M. RUDRA KUMAR

Rudra Kumar holds a PhD degree in Computer Science and Engineering on the topic entitled" Maintenance of Software Artifacts Using Machine Learning Approaches" and is with Annamacharya Institute of Technology & Sciences (an Autonomous Institute), Rajampet, A.P., India working as Professor and Head Dept. of CSE. He is chairman of the BOS of the Department and also held a position as the Academic Council Member of the Institute. His research interests include Machine Learning, Computer Vision methods and Biomedical Image Processing. He is a member of various professional bodies and published a good number of papers in refereed journals. He acted as Jury in various National Seminars and presented his research articles in reputed conferences.

www.ingramcontent.com/pod-product-compliance
Lightning Source LLC
Chambersburg PA
CBHW052149070326
40689CB00050B/2871